Polaroid Guest

Celebrating

Design For Life

Made in the USA
Middletown, DE
23 January 2020

83613771R00066